Recipes for Fitness
for Very Busy People

How to prepare slimming "Spa Food" in your own home in the quickest and easiest possible way.

by Eleanor Brown

Art Work by Kathleen Goolsby

Published by:
FITNESS PUBLICATIONS
1991 Country Place
Ojai, California 93023

About the Author:

Eleanor Brown developed the well known and popular Spa Cuisine that is served at The Oaks at Ojai and The Palms at Palm Springs.

She constantly reads, studies and attends seminars on nutrition to update the spa food.

Her recipes have been featured in Glamour Magazine, Better Homes and Gardens, Palm Springs Life, the Los Angeles Times Home Magazine, the Ladies Home Journal and numerous other publications.

Eleanor's Spa Cuisine is offered in her cooking classes at Ventura College, Moorpark College, the Learning Network and many private clubs and groups.

She has done Food Consulting with Measurex Corporation, adding Spa Cuisine to their staff dining room, as well as the Sierra Summit Ski Camp, the Santa Maria Inn and Advanced Computer Communications, Inc. and numerous restaurants.

She writes a food column for the Ojai Valley News and her other publications include: *Recipes for Fitness from The Palms at Palm Springs* and *Fitness Recipes from The Oaks at Ojai.*

She has also demonstrated Spa Style Cooking on numerous TV shows and videos . . . The latest being a Spa Style video by McGraw-Hill.

This book is dedicated to all the wonderful guests at The Oaks at Ojai and The Palms at Palm Springs whose more than enthusiastic reception of my other publications, along with requests for "MORE," inspired this book.

To my husband, Stan, who helped in all ways; typing, editing, tasting, encouraging and, sometimes, criticizing.

To Sheila Cluff who has always encouraged and helped me to grow.

And to everyone who thinks they haven't the time to shop, cook and eat for FITNESS.

Table of Contents

Introduction

Chapter 1   THE BUSY PERSONS RECIPE FOR FITNESS 2
Why diets don't work and a plan for permanent weight control.

Chapter 2   ORGANIZING THE BUSY PERSONS KITCHEN 6
Stock your staples and make sure you've got the equipment that makes food preparation fun and easy.

Chapter 3   ORGANIZING THE BUSY PERSONS MENU AND SHOPPING LIST 10
How to make up your menu and make it work for you so that your shopping list almost prepares itself.

Chapter 4   ORGANIZING THE BUSY PERSONS SHOPPING AND COOKING 12
How to use a block of time just once a week so that most of your cooking is done.

Chapter 5   SAUCES, DRESSING, DIPS AND SPREADS
These are the basics that save you calories everyday. Keep some on hand in your refrigerator.
BLUE CHEESE DRESSING 14
CREAMY CHEESE 15
CREAMY MAYONNAISE 16
CREAMY ORANGE PEANUT BUTTER 17
FRESH CRANBERRY-ORANGE RELISH 18
HOT ARTICHOKE-CHILI DIP 19
ITALIAN SAUCE 20
LOW CAL SOUR CREAM TARTAR SAUCE,
   FRUIT DRESSING & HERB DRESSING 21
NON-FAT WHIPPED CREAM 22
REAL BUTTER DECALORIZED 23
SIMPLE SALSA 24

Chapter 6   **BETTER BREADS AND MAGNIFICIENT MUFFINS**
Good tasting and satisfying breads that are easy to prepare.
BANANA BRAN MUFFIN 25
BLUEBERRY MUFFINS 26
CHIPS FOR DIPS 27
(Seasoned Potato Chips & Tortilla Chips)
CORNBREAD 28
CREATIVE CREPES 29
DATE NUT BREAD 30
ELEANOR'S EASIEST BREAD 31
ORANGE-OAT MUFFINS 32
WHOLE WHEAT POPOVERS 33

Chapter 7   **SENSATIONAL SOUPS**
To begin the meal or serve as the meal itself. Be sure to make some for the freezer.
ALBONDEGAS SOUP 34
CREAM OF CARROT SOUP 35
LENTIL-BARLEY MEAL IN A BOWL 36
MUSHROOM-TOFU SOUP 37
QUICKEST MINESTRONE 38
SHERRIED GREEN PEA SOUP 39
VICHYSSOISE 40

Chapter 8   **SUPER SALADS**
Some of these make a delicious meal in a bowl.
BROCCOLI SALAD 41
CRAB STUFFED ARTICHOKE or TOMATO 42
CREAMY CUCUMBER MOLD 43
CAULIFLOWER-BEET SALAD 44
GREEN BEAN SALAD 44
GREEN PEA SALAD WITH CURRIED ORANGE
    YOGURT SAUCE 46

MARINATED CARROT SALAD 47
MARINATED TOFU SALAD 48
PASTA SALAD 49
SALAD NICCOISE 50
SHRIMP SLAW SUPREME 51
SHRIMP STUFFED PAPAYA 52
TABOULI 53

Chapter 9   VEGIES AND VEGIE MAIN DISHES
Use lots of these. They tend to be high in fiber, low in fat and full of the vita-
mins and minerals that keep your immune system functioning well.

BAKED YAM PUFF 54
BROILED TOMATO PARMESAN 55
ELLY'S QUICK VEGETARIAN CHILI 56
FAST FETTUCINI PRIMAVERA 57
FROSTED CAULIFLOWER 58
MAGIC MACARONI AND CHEESE 59
OVEN-FRIED ONION RINGS 60
PITA PIZZA 61
SIMPLE STUFFED ACORN SQUASH 62
SPINACH WITH ONION 63
SPEEDY SPINACH WITH ONION 63
WILD RICE PILAF 64
ZUCCHINI SAUTE and/or ZUCCHINI FRITTATA 65

Chapter 10   PLEASING POULTRY AND SUMPTUOUS SEAFOOD
Quality protein with very little fat.

CASHEW CHICKEN WITH TOFU 66
CHICKEN FRICASSE 67
CHICKEN RELLENO 68
CRAB QUICHE 69
FISH FILLETS BAKED IN YOGURT SAUCE 70
OVEN-"FRIED" CHICKEN BREASTS 71

POLLA PICATA 72

QUICK TURKEY PARMESAN 73

TURKEY DIVAN 74

TURKEY KABOB 75

TURKEY TOFU STROGANOFF 76

Chapter 11   **DELICIOUS DESSERTS**
Under 100 calories a serving! They'll never believe it.

AMBROSIA 77

APPLE BROWN BETTY 78

CAROB-PEANUT BUTTER MOUSSE 79

CHIFFON ''PUMPKIN'' PIE 80

EIGHT PRECIOUS PUDDING 81

FRUIT WHIP 82

ORANGE OAT COOKIES 83

PERMISIMMON FRUIT CAKE 84

POPCORN 85
(Honey Corn, Carmel Corn, Seasoned Corn)

SHERRIED PEAR 86

WINTER FRUIT COMPOTE 87

Introduction

I am writing this book eight years after publishing "Fitness Recipes from The Oaks at Ojai" and five years after "Recipes for Fitness from The Palms at Palm Springs." In my work as District (Foods) Manager, floating between the two health resorts, I have met many of you busy, goal-oriented people and your response to my other publications has been more than gratifying. However, the message I've been getting from you lately goes like this:

"Eleanor, I've bought all of your recipes and they're great. And I love the food at The Oaks and The Palms . . . BUT . . . I can't seem to get myself organized to cook. So I wind up buying a hamburger, pizza or some fried chicken on my way home from work."

This book, "Recipes for Fitness for Very Busy People" has been written to satisfy your needs and to help you get both your KITCHEN and your LIFE organized so that you can be the very best that you can be. In the chapter "The Busy Person's Recipe for Fitness," you'll find a simple plan for weight control that works. The chapters on "Getting Organized" will give you some ideas that should help you organize your kitchen, your shopping and your cooking.

The recipes in this book are most of the 'guest tested' favorites that I've developed since my other publications. However, since this book is for very busy people, I've revised many of the recipes to make them quicker and easier. To do this, I have sometimes used canned or frozen vegetables. Even though I prefer fresh, you'll still be better off using a few shortcuts than living on high fat, salty fast foods.

Many of the recipes include the use of Dr. Jensen's Broth Powder which is a favorite seasoning at The Oaks and The Palms. If your Health Food Store doesn't carry it, you can order it from The Oaks or use your own favorite bouillon or broth mixture.

Each recipe gives an activity that will burn the calories in a serving of that particular recipe. This is to increase your awareness that calories which are not used will be stored as FAT. When I speak of calories the numbers are always an approximation.

Between these covers, you'll find many suggestions for the shopping, cooking, eating and exercising ingredients of your "Recipe for Fitness." However, I don't believe that anyone can be at their total best without nurturing their spiritual nature. Do allow time, each day, for a quiet time, a prayer time, a time to get centered and thank God for the blessings in your life and enlist his aid in solving problems . . . and may God bless you in your efforts to be the very best you can be!

The Busy Person's Recipe for Fitness

Diets don't work. If diets really worked, every magazine in every store wouldn't have the ultimate, new diet, designed to melt away those excess pounds and inches, as if by magic. We all want to believe in magic and instant weight loss, but we know better. If there were an immediate and "no work" method of being thin, would we be an overweight society?

In this chapter, my goal is to absolutely convince you that diets don't work so that you really never will go on another diet. Going on a diet means eventually going off a diet. Going off of a diet is almost always followed by a weight gain which triggers the whole miserable yo-yo syndrome of losing and gaining the same ten or twenty pounds. When you "go on a diet," you generally feel deprived. You often feel that you deserve to be punished because you feel guilty for overeating and gaining the weight in the first place. The more rigid the diet, the more you tend to become obsessed with food . . . especially food expressly forbidden on your particular diet.

This is one of the reasons why I don't believe in diets. We all have different foods that are important to us and if we're told to give them up, we feel deprived and this is one of the things that sets us up for diet failure. I do believe in cutting out as much fat, salt and sugar as possible and finding palatable substitutes for favorite foods which are high in those ingredients.

When you diet and drastically reduce calories, your metabolism slows down as your body struggles to maintain itself. Therefore, you go off the diet with a slower metabolism and that is part of the reason for the rapid weight gain after the diet. However, the biggest reason for the weight gain after that period of self denial and deprivation that we call dieting is that you haven't made any permanent changes in your eating habits or in your life style. I have never met anyone who lost weight and kept it off without making permanent changes.

One day, on a brisk walk at The Palms, one of our lovely, trim guests assured me that she had lost weight on a diet and kept if off. However, as our walk and talk progressed, I learned that she had never gone off the diet. In other words, her "diet" was not a diet at all, but a permanent change in her eating habits. Also, this guest is extremely committed to regular aerobic exercise.

Because we feel constantly deprived while on most diets, stressful situations tend to cause a "binge," followed by feelings of guilt and a loss of self esteem. This is the point at which most diets are abandoned. See if this story sounds like anyone you know.

"Pleasingly Plump Patty" has failed at many diets but dreams of finding the one perfect diet that will give her the figure she has envied in others and wanted for herself. One day, while standing in line at the supermarket, she notices that the latest copy of "Forever Thin" magazine is featuring the sensational new Death Valley Diet that all of her friends have been using while losing. Patty feels a flicker of hope and buys the magazine. She quickly checks the diet and purchases a lot of tuna, cottage cheese, lettuce, pickles, artificial sweeteners and diet drinks. She starts the diet with high hopes, visualizing her plumpness being replaced with a flat stomach and no thighs. She weighs and measures portions of tuna and cottage cheese while dreaming of pizza and ice cream. She is losing weight but she is feeling very deprived. Then, one night, when Patty is very hungry and has dinner all ready, her husband is late and doesn't call. As she waits, her hunger increases and to it are added feelings of anger, hurt and frustration. At this point, she decides to eat just one cookie (food is a tranquilizer) and before she knows it, she has eaten all the cookies. She now feels guilt along with her anger, hurt and frustration. She's hurting so much that she looks for more food to make her feel better, so she eats everything in sight. When poor Patty's husband finally appears, she is too embarrassed to tell him about her binge, so she sits down and eats with him. The next morning, her scale shows a big weight gain and that's the end of the diet. Patty has added to her long list of diet failures with the usual loss of self esteem and the rapid weight gain, accompanied by a slower metabolism. She had lost some fat, some water and some muscle. She gains back water weight and more fat, which increases her tendency to get fat. Patty is on a negative cycle and has taken another step toward obesity.

If diets don't work, does this mean that fat people are doomed to eternal fatness? Absolutely not! I'm going to give you a plan for making small, but important, lifestyle changes that will produce a slow but permanent fat loss. You'll lose weight too but the most important change will be your fat and inch loss. This plan involves exercise which will help produce a gain in muscle mass as you lose fat. Muscle weighs over twice as much as fat but it doesn't take up nearly as much space. You can actually get into a smaller size without showing a weight loss on the scale.

To lose a pound of fat in a week, you've got to get rid of 3,500 calories which you can do by burning them or cutting them out of your eating habits. If we divide the seven days in a week into 3,500, we get 500 calories a day. If you will burn an extra 250 calories a day (preferably in an aerobic type exercise) and cut 250 food calories a day, you should lose a pound a week . . . or fifty two pounds in a year! When you arrive at your 'set point,' you'll probably find that you level off and stay at that weight very easily. Since you haven't gone on a diet, there is no diet to go off of, so the weight loss is permanent. After a very social weekend, you'll probably show a weight gain but by simply returning to your normally good habits, you'll return to your 'set point.'

Let's take poor, unfortunate, Patty, last heard of binging and heading toward real obesity. Patty thinks she hates exercise but she visits The Palms, The Oaks or reads a book by Covert Bailey or Dr. Kenneth Cooper and she is very surprised to find that she doesn't have to work as hard as she had feared to exercise in her 'fat burning training zone.' She gets into a walking program, walking briskly for an hour each morning. She is burning a good 250 calories on her walk and her metabolism is raised as a result of that walk, so that her body burns calories faster for several extra hours. Patty also finds that she feels calmer, brighter and more energetic. She is able to accomplish more in less time and, if her husband is late and forgets to call, she maintains her self control. If he's really late, she takes another walk and finds that the walking has a very calming effect. She is feeling very good about herself and her world. Along with her walking program, Patty is learning to save 250 calories each day by choosing foods with less fat. The quality of her life improves and before she knows it, she's wearing a smaller size and her friends are commenting on her trim figure. They all think that she's lost more weight than she has. That's the 500 plan.

$$
\begin{array}{r}
250 \text{ calories burned} \\
+ \quad 250 \text{ calories cut} \\
\hline
500 \text{ calories per day.} \\
\times 7 \text{ days in a week} \\
\hline
\end{array}
$$

3500 calories a week or a loss of a pound a week.
Remember that you won't see it all on the scale.
Some of it will show in inches lost.

I frequently give talks on this subject and it is interesting to observe the audience reaction. "Eric von Portly" has a million reasons for not finding the time to exercise while "Trim Tina," who lives in the city with smog in the air and muggers on every street, never misses her morning exercise. She goes to her gym three mornings a week and jumps on a trampoline or rides her exercise bike on the other mornings. If she misses an occasional morning, she takes a walk at lunch time. Tina has to get up at 5:00 a.m. to have time to exercise and get ready for work, but it's worth it.

Do remember that the food you eat must be used or stored as fat. One of the incredibly efficient aspects of our bodies is this ability to store excess fuel in the form of fat. This insures our ability to survive famine. However, since, in our society, we experience so few famines, I'm sure you'll want to get on an aerobic program and learn to work in your Training Zone to burn fat more efficiently. This is the most important behavior change that you can make to insure that you'll never diet again. After all, as a very busy person, you don't have the time to invest in diets that don't work.

Organizing the Busy Person's Kitchen

The condition of your kitchen is most important because if it's well organized and well equipped, you'll truly enjoy cooking. And we're all more likely to do the things we enjoy. Let's begin by checking your equipment.

I'm not going to list the obvious equipment that every kitchen has in it. If you don't have basic kitchen equipment you very likely would have little interest in this book. I'm going to suggest some equipment that will make your life easier and shorten the time spent in preparation.

1. **FOOD PROCESSOR** — This is essential for making "CREAMY CHEESE," (my favorite calorie saver). You can mix muffins or bread in it, too.

2. **MICROWAVE OVEN** — The best way to heat leftovers, which, as a very busy person you definitely want to do.

3. **BLENDER** — The ideal way to prepare "breakfast in a glass" which very busy people frequently do.

4. **CROCK POT** — This enables you to walk in the door to the aroma of dinner cooking. A delightful experience!

5. **HOT AIR POPPER** — This is for making popcorn without fat. There is also a microwave pan for this.

6. **HAND MIXER** — This adds the volume to non-fat whipped cream and lo-cal butter.

7. **MUFFIN TINS** — Get the ones with 1/3 cup capacity because my muffin recipes are planned to make small muffins.

8. **MAGNETIC NOTE PAD** — Keep this attached to your refrigerator so that you'll keep a running list as you run out of staples.

9. **STEAMER BASKET** — Or 4 qt. kettle with a rack, for steaming anything.

10. **GLASS MEASURING CUPS** — With handles and pouring lips.

Staples are the things you always try to keep in your kitchen. With them, you can prepare a quick meal or fitness snack. Here is my list. You'll add or subtract, according to your individual taste and preference.

Herbs, Spices, Seasonings and Condiments

JENSEN'S BROTH POWDER   Use as a soup stock or seasoning.

BASIL   Outstanding on tomato and summer squash.

CHILI POWDER   A must for Mexican food.

CINNAMON   A natural sweetener. Wonderful with apple, yam and winter squash.

CUMIN (ground)   Great in Mexican, Indian and Oriental dishes.

CURRY POWDER   The basic for Indian cooking. Use very small amounts to begin with.

DILL WEED (dried)   Enhances almost any vegetable.

GARLIC (dried or fresh)   Enlivens most salads and sauces for Italian, Mexican, Indian and Oriental cuisines.

HONEY   A sweeter sweetener than granulated sugar. Use it sparingly.

LEMON (fresh)   Enhances the flavor of almost anything. Use to dilute heavy dressings and cut calories while improving flavor.

MARJORAM   Good on tomatoes, potatoes and peas.

MUSTARD (dried)   Use in CREAMY MAYONNAISE and other salad dressings.

NUTMEG (ground)   Use in curry, muffins and cookies.

OIL (safflower & olive)   Use in smallest amounts for light dressings and sauteing.

ONION (fresh & dried)	Use in most ethnic cooking and salads.
OREGANO (dried)	A must in Italian and Mexican cuisine.
MOLASSES (blackstrap)	A most nutritious sweetener. Strong but good in bran muffins.
PAPRIKA	Use it to give color to pale dishes, like cauliflower.
PEPPERCORNS (ground)	Use in soups and sauces, to taste.
SESAME SEEDS	Wonderful on breads and toasted on Oriental dishes.
SOY SAUCE	A must in Oriental cooking. Find a low sodium brand.
THYME	Use in Italian sauce and on vegetables.
VINEGAR	Cider, wine and some of the new gourmet varieties. Raspberry is wonderful. Use in marinades and dressings.
WINE	Chablis, Burgundy, Sherry and Dry Vermouth. They are wonderful for no-salt cooking. Most of the calories cook away.

Some other items that I keep on hand are:

Unsalted butter	Various herb teas
Eggs	Coffee
Whole wheat flour	Whole grain crackers
Rice flour	Whole wheat mini-pita bread

Oatmeal	Yeast
Raw Bran	Lentils
Powdered Non-Fat Milk	Barley
Brown rice	Split Peas
Wild rice	Frozen orange juice
Bulgur	Low-fat cheeses (Mozzarella, Jarlsburg, Cheddar)
* Tomato Paste (unsalted)	I use _Lifetime Cheese_ with 50% less fat and salt
Non-fat yogurt	Cottage cheese
	Parmesan cheese

If you'll take the time to stock your kitchen with good equipment and staples and restock your staples as needed, you're on the way to being organized.

*Since it is often difficult to find unsalted tomato juice and sauce, stock your pantry with tomato paste and save money and space.

For Tomato Sauce

1 part **TOMATO PASTE**
1 part **WATER**
Combine and mix well.

For Tomato Juice

1 part **TOMATO PASTE**
2 parts **WATER**
Combine and mix well. Taste and add water as needed.

Organizing The Busy Person's Menu & Shopping List

Right here is where you win or loose in your quest to be in control of what you are going to eat. You must have a menu and a shopping list. Both can be very flexible but they are absolutely necessary before you venture out to the market. Your list will save you money and time and you'll eat better than you've ever eaten in your life.

Here is the way to do it. Sit down with your datebook or calendar, your list of required staples and your favorite cookbook (I hope it's one of mine). Also be aware of what you have in your freezer and refrigerator. Check the newspaper ads from your market. Usually the produce that's on sale is at its peak and purchasing the 'specials' can save you many dollars.

Check your calendar and count how many dinners you'll eat at home. (Did you ever buy a lot of beautiful fresh vegetables, take them home to your refrigerator and then discover them rotting a week later because you weren't home for any dinners?) Your calendar should also be your key to what kind of meals you'll be wanting and how many people you'll be feeding.

Now you're ready to plan a menu and from your menu, your shopping list will almost prepare itself.

Here is the way my menu planning and shopping list develop:

Breakfast is usually a 'superdrink' (this is 2 T. of Brewer's Yeast and 1/4 C. of Non-fat Powdered Milk blended into Orange Juice), a muffin and coffee. Since the muffins are made ahead, that gets us out the door in a hurry.

Lunch is usually fresh fruit and cottage cheese or a vegetable salad with whole grain crackers, or I'm out to lunch.

So, except for fresh fruit and salad vegetables, breakfast and lunch are pretty well taken care of with the staples. That leaves dinners and a typical week might look like this:

My Sample Menu

SUNDAY: My night to have dinner and lecture at The Oaks. Stan can quickly make a great Pita Bread Salad and he can microwave a large soup mug of frozen minestrone for his dinner.

MONDAY: Green salad with blue cheese dressing, Chicken Fricasse, Eleanor's Easiest Bread and Red Grapes for dessert.

TUESDAY: Lettuce and sliced tomatoes, steamed vegies with Mozzarella, baked yam and fresh pear.

WEDNESDAY: Cauliflower-beet salad, Chicken Relleno, tortilla chips and fresh banana sliced on-to pineapple chunks for dessert.

THURSDAY: Pita Salad, Lentil-Barley casserole and Frosted Pears.

FRIDAY: Green Bean Salad, quick Turkey Parmesan, baked Yam Puff, Speedy Spinach with onion and fresh pineapple.

SATURDAY: Company! So it's dinner for four:
Hot Artichoke-Chili Dip with raw vegetables and whole grain crackers. Broccoli Salad, Crab Quiche with Broiled Tomato and Wild Rice Pilaf. Eleanor's Easiest Bread and fresh pears, frosted or sherried.

My Shopping List

3	Chicken Breasts	1	lb. Broccoli	Lettuce
1	package Sliced Turkey Breasts	1/2	lb. Cherry Tomatoes	1/2 lb. Tomatoes
1	package Frozen Crab Meat	4	Yams	Pears
2	oz. package of Blue Cheese	1	Cauliflower	Grapes
1	small can Green Chilis	1/2	lb. Green Beans	Fresh Pineapple
1	can Artichoke Hearts		Carrots	Bananas
1	package Frozen Spinach		Potatoes	
1	can Beets		Small head Celery	

Added to this list would be the staples listed on my magnetic note pad.

Organizing the Busy Person's Shopping and Cooking

Now you're ready to go shopping. However, your once-a-week shopping must not be a quick run to the store and then home to throw the food into cupboards and refrigerator. Shop at a time when you don't have to battle crowds and when you can take the food to your kitchen and do most of your preparation as you put the food away. Thus, you invest a block of time, just once a week and come home every day to dinners that are almost ready. No more going to the store or the local 'Fast Food Emporium' after work . . . Just good food, well prepared, for less money.

Now let's take my menu and buy the food and see how we'll handle it when we get to my kitchen.

Here is the food preparation I would do while I put away my groceries. This will result in a week of nutritious and delicious meals with very little cooking left to do. This shopping would be done very early on Monday morning when you have the store to yourself. If you must do your shopping on the weekend, at least go very early or very, very late . . . that's the only way to avoid crowds on weekends.

1. Put all vegetables in the sink to be washed.
2. Put fruit in attractive bowls. Ripe fruit goes directly into the refrigerator and the 'not-so-ripe' fruit is left out.
3. Turn on oven and mix Eleanor's Easiest Bread and leave rising in a warm place.
4. Wash and trim the vegetables, cutting some for 'steamed vegetables,' putting some in the Crock Pot and readying some for use in salads. I put my vegies for steamed vegetables right into the ramekins used for serving. The ramekins go right into a plastic bag and are ready for the microwave. Vegetable trimmings go into your stock pot and if you don't have a stock pot, don't feel guilty. Many people don't.
5. Assemble Chicken Fricasse and leave cooking in the crock pot.
6. Crisp tortilla chips in oven which is heating to bake your bread.
7. Pound parmesan cheese into sliced turkey breast, wrap in wax paper and keep in meat drawer for your Quick Turkey Parmesan.
8. Thaw the crab meat, assemble and partly bake quiche for Saturday's dinner party.
9. Mix Blue Cheese dressing.
10. Bake bread and cut in half (or make two small loaves).
11. Make sure you have "Calorie Savers" on hand and make any you need, such as Lo-Cal Butter, Creamy Cheese or Creamy Mayonnaise.

12. If you have no Mexican Sauce on hand, make sauce for Chicken Relleno. (Make extra and freeze some for next time.)
13. If you have no Lentil-Barley soup in your freezer, assemble it (about 5 minutes) and freeze some.

After completing all of that you're ready for the week and it's a wonderful feeling to finally get organized. It will take an hour and a half to two hours, depending upon your skills. You'll save time, money, calories and nutrients by investing a good chunk of time once a week. Such a bargain!

Now, let's go back to my menu and see just how easy the week will be.

SUNDAY: Stan puts soup mug in the microwave, heats the Pita Bread and fills it with lettuce and tomato, dressed with Creamy Mayonnaise.

MONDAY: Thicken the Chicken Fricasse gravy, slice bread and toss already washed lettuce with Blue Cheese dressing. Wash the grapes.

TUESDAY: Bake yam in microwave for 15 minutes. Slice tomato. Put vegies in microwave and top with Mozzarella for the last minute . . . or steam in the steamer. Wash the pears.

WEDNESDAY: Use steamed cauliflower from Tuesday and combine with canned beets for salad. Assemble Chili Relleno, using leftover chicken from the fricasse. Slice pineapple and bananas. (In a pinch you might use 'No Sugar' canned pineapple.)

THURSDAY: Heat Lentil-Barley casserole (add any desired leftover vegetables) and make Pita Salads while casserole heats.

FRIDAY: Use leftover baked yams to assemble 'puff.' Mix the thawed spinach with chopped onion and heat while Turkey Parmesan sautes.

SATURDAY: Use broccoli from steamed vegies for salad. Take Wild Rice Pilaf from freezer (or make it early in the morning). Heat the dip and serve. Heat the quiche and wild rice. Heat bread, wrapped in foil, in oven and slice. Broil tomato just before serving. If serving sherried pears, bake in the morning. If 'frosted,' just cut, core and frost the cut side with Creamy Cheese.

Bon Appetite!

Blue Cheese Dressing

Makes 2 1/2 Cups   33 Calories per ounce

3/4	C.	BUTTERMILK
3/4	C.	LOW-FAT COTTAGE CHEESE
3/4	C.	NON-FAT YOGURT
2	oz.	BLUE CHEESE
1	tsp.	GARLIC POWDER
1/4	tsp.	BLACK PEPPER
1	tsp.	DRIED ONION FLAKES

Combine all ingredients in a blender or bowl. Blend until well mixed but not completely smooth.

Use as a dip or dressing. This is very good poured over a wedge of lettuce . . . which is just about as quick and easy as a salad can be.

Practice playing the piano for just eight minutes and you've burned an ounce of this great dressing.

Creamy Cheese

Makes 1 Cup   20 Calories per tablespoon

3/4   C.   **LOW-FAT COTTAGE CHEESE**
1/4   C.   **MOZZARELLA, JARLSBURG, SHARP CHEDDAR, CAMEMBERT** (or your favorite cheese).
Combine cheeses in food processor and process until creamy. Use as is or add your favorite herbs.

This is my favorite calorie saver because cheese is my favorite snack. It is extremely simple to prepare in a food processor and at 20 calories per tablespoon you'll save approximately 60 calories an ounce if you choose to eat 2 tablespoons of the mix rather than an ounce of most other cheeses.

Store in a crock in your refrigerator and use as a calorie saving snack, stuffed into mushrooms, celery, or spread on apple or pear slices. You can also spread it on whole grain crackers. Formed into tiny balls and rolled in toasted sesame seeds it makes an outstanding hors d'oeuvre. Try just mashing it into a baked potato for a dinner treat. If it is melted over low heat it makes a delightful cream sauce.

A tablespoon of this can be burned on a ten minute stroll.

Creamy Mayonnaise

Makes approx. 1 3/4 Cups   20 Calories per tablespoon

1		**EGG**
1 1/3	C.	**COTTAGE CHEESE**
2	tsp.	**RED WINE VINEGAR**
1	T.	**LEMON JUICE**
1/2	tsp.	**DRY MUSTARD**

Combine in blender and process until smooth.

1	T.	**SAFFLOWER OIL**

Add with blender running.

The addition of a bit of oil gives this low calorie version of mayonnaise the texture of the real thing. Meanwhile you save 80 calories per tablespoon.

Just five minutes of typing will burn the calories in a tablespoon of this really good mayonnaise.

16

Creamy Orange Peanut Butter

Makes 1 1/4 Cups   **16 Calories per tablespoon**

1	C.	**LOW-FAT COTTAGE CHEESE**
2	T.	**PEANUT BUTTER (UNSALTED)**
2	T.	**FROZEN ORANGE JUICE CONCENTRATE**

Combine in the food processor and process until smooth.

This is a super dip for carrots, celery and apple slices. Make open faced sandwiches and garnish with grated carrot or sliced apple.

If you leave out the peanut butter, you'll have a lovely fresh tasting spread or dip. You'll also save half of the calories.

You can burn the calories in a tablespoon of the peanut butter version if you spend a couple of minutes splitting wood.

Fresh Cranberry-Orange Relish

Serving size is 1/4 Cup   7 Calories per serving

3	C.	**FRESH CRANBERRIES**
1		**LARGE ORANGE** (cut into chunks with skin)
2		**RED APPLES** (quartered and cut in chunks)

Process in food processor until coarsely chopped, using ON-OFF switch. Place in a covered bowl and chill.

2 to 4 T.   **HONEY**
Add honey to taste and serve.

This will add a lovely fresh accent to your next turkey dinner. We serve it with Rock Cornish game hen at The Oaks and The Palms every Thanksgiving and Christmas.

You'll burn those 7 calories playing cards for just seven minutes (especially if you are loosing).

18

Hot Artichoke-Chili Dip

Makes 1 1/2 cups   15 Calories per tablespoon

1   Can   **ARTICHOKE HEARTS** (drained)
           Process smooth in food processor.

1 small can **GREEN CHILIS** (chopped)
4   oz.   **LOW-FAT CHEDDAR CHEESE** (grated)
           Mix into artichoke puree.

Place in small crocks. (Freeze any that you won't be using.) To serve, heat through in oven or microwave until cheese melts.

Serve with vegetables, whole grain crackers or 'Chips for Dips.'

This freezes well and makes a hit with guests. There's something impressive about a hot hors d'oeuvre. I well remember being impressed, thinking it was the best dip I'd ever tasted when our "super gourmet friends," the Burgners, served this at their Palm Desert Home.

Italian Sauce

Makes 4 Cups

40 Calories per 1/2 C. serving

2 2/3	C.	**TOMATO PUREE**
2/3	C.	**DRY RED WINE**
2	T.	**MINCED OLIVES**

Bring to a boil in a kettle.

1	**ONION** (chopped)
1	**GREEN PEPPER** (chopped)
2	**GARLIC CLOVES** (chopped)

Peel and chop vegetables. Add to boiling sauce and reduce to simmer.

1	tsp.	**OREGANO**
1	tsp.	**BASIL**
1/2	tsp.	**THYME**
1/2	tsp.	**MARJORAM**

Grind in mortar and pestle. Add to sauce and simmer for 1 hour or until desired consistency is reached.

Use this for a quick English muffin or Pita bread pizza, with any pasta dish or to add an Italian flavor to steamed vegetables. You can make a wonderful low calorie lasagna, using this sauce and a cottage cheese filling.

You can burn the calories in a whole half cup of this sauce by simply doing some mending for 20 minutes.

20

Low Cal Sour Cream Tartar Sauce
Fruit Dressing & Herb Dressing

Makes one Pint   **15 Calories per tablespoon**

For Sour Cream

1 1/2	C.	**LOW-FAT COTTAGE CHEESE**
1/2	C.	**BUTTERMILK**
1	tsp.	**FRESH LEMON JUICE**

Combine in blender and blend until smooth and creamy. Used as sour cream. It's wonderful on a baked potato.

For Tartar Sauce

1/4	C.	**DRIED BELL PEPPER**
1/4	C.	**DRIED ONION**
1 1/2	tsp.	**RED WINE VINEGAR**
1/4	tsp.	**DRY MUSTARD**
1/4	tsp.	**CREAM OF TARTAR**
1	T.	**LEMON JUICE**

Add to sour cream, blend and chill at least 2 hours to thicken. This is delicious.

For Fruit Dressing

2	T.	**FROZEN ORANGE CONCENTRATE**
1	tsp.	**CURRY POWDER** (optional)

Add to sour cream, blend and chill. Use as a dip or dressing for fruit.

For Herb Dressing

1		**CHOPPED SCALLION**
1	T.	**FRESH PARSLEY**
1/8	tsp.	**DILL WEED**
1	tsp.	**ONION POWDER**

Add to sour cream in blender and blend until smooth. Chill. Use as a dressing or dip for vegetables.

Burn the calories in a tablespoon of this mix while knitting for just seven minutes.

Non-Fat Whipped Cream

Makes 2 Cups   **20 Calories per 1/4 Cup**

1/2	tsp.	**UNFLAVORED GELATIN**
1	T.	**WATER**

Place water in a small pan and sprinkle gelatin on water to soak. After all gelatin powder has soaked in, stir over low heat until clear. Cool.

1/4	C.	**NON-FAT POWDERED MILK**
1/2	C.	**ICED WATER**
1/2	tsp.	**HONEY**
1/2	tsp.	**VANILLA**

Combine in large bowl and whip in gelatin mixture. Whip until light and fluffy and resembles whipped cream.

This can be used as a topping or as the base for a pudding. Or layer it with fruit sauce for a pretty parfait.

You'll burn the calories in a fourth cup of this during the 10 minutes you'll stand while you prepare it.

22

Real Butter Decalorized

Makes approximately 2 Cups

35 Calories/tablespoon
10 Calories/teaspoon

1/4	lb.	**SWEET BUTTER**
3/4	C.	**BUTTERMILK**

Leave butter and buttermilk at room temperature to soften the butter and remove the chill from the buttermilk. Place butter in 4 cup measure or small deep bowl. Whip with electric hand mixer and slowly add the buttermilk. When the butter will not absorb any more buttermilk, pour off the remainder and you should have at least 3 times as much butter as you originally had.

This recipe saves dollars as well as calories. Store in a crock and cover or if your family is small, freeze a portion. Use as a spread on vegetables or for broiling fish. It has a smooth buttery flavor but much less fat than the original butter. Keep this in your refrigerator to save fat calories every day.

Seven minutes of window cleaning will burn those 35 calories and improve your outlook on life.

Simple Salsa

Makes 1 1/2 Cups

6 Calories per ounce

1/2	C.	**TOMATO SAUCE**
1	C.	**TOMATOES**

Chop tomatoes coarsely and combine with the tomato juice.

1/2	C.	**GREEN CHILES**

Cut chiles in 1/4'' pieces.

1/4	C.	**GREEN ONIONS**
1	T.	**RED WINE VINEGAR**
1	tsp.	**JENSEN'S BROTH POWDER**

Mince onions fine. Combine ingredients. Hand mix, leaving chunks of tomato visible and chill your salsa.

Serve this with your favorite Mexican dishes. We top our tostadas with it at The Oaks and The Palms. Try combining this with avocado and creamy mayonnaise for a great guacamole.

You can burn the 6 calories in an ounce of this while you tidy your desk for three minutes (sitting down).

Banana Bran Muffin

Makes 24 muffins   **70 Calories per muffin**

1	C.	**RAISINS**
1	C.	**BOILING WATER**

Pour boiling water over raisins and soak 15 minutes.

1	C.	**WHOLE WHEAT FLOUR**
2	C.	**RAW BRAN**
1	tsp.	**BAKING SODA**

Combine in a large bowl

1 1/2	C.	**BUTTERMILK**
1	C.	**MASHED BANANA**
1	tsp.	**VANILLA**
1/4	C.	**FROZEN APPLE CONCENTRATE**
3		**EGG YOLKS**

Combine in blender and process until smooth.

3		**EGG WHITES**

Whip stiff. Add blender contents to bran mixture and mix just enough to combine.
Fold whipped egg white into batter. Drain raisins and fold into batter.

Spoon lightly into a non-stick sprayed muffin tin. Bake at 400º for 20 minutes.

This muffin is a favorite with guests and staff at the Palms.

Burn the calories in one muffin on an easy 25 minute bike ride.

Blueberry Muffins

Makes 24 muffins   60 Calories per muffin

2	C.	**RAW BRAN**
1	C.	**ROLLED OATS**
1/4	C.	**WHOLE WHEAT FLOUR**
2	tsp.	**CINNAMON**
1	tsp.	**NUTMEG**

Combine in a large bowl.

2		**EGGS (BEATEN)**
1	C.	**BUTTERMILK**
1/4	C.	**BLACK STRAP MOLASSES**
1/4	C.	**SUNFLOWER SEEDS**

Combine, add to bran mixture and mix lightly.

2   **BLUEBERRIES**

Spoon lightly into non-stick muffin tins. Bake at 350º for 40 minutes or until brown.

I like to keep muffins always on hand for our favorite breakfast of a muffin and fresh fruit. I save time by making a large batch of muffins and lining my muffin tins with cup cake papers to save dish washing time.

Have fun on an easy horseback ride while you burn the 60 calories contained in one of these good tasting, good for you muffins.

Chips for Dips

Seasoned Potato Chips

Makes 6 servings   Approximately 60 Calories for 8 chips

3   **RAW POTATOES** (scrubbed)
           Wash & slice wafer thin. Place on cookie sheet which has been sprayed with non-stick vegetable spray.

1   tsp. **ONION POWDER**
1   tsp. **PAPRIKA**
1/2 tsp. **CURRY POWDER**
1   tsp. **DR. JENSEN'S BROTH POWDER**
           Combine & sprinkle generously on potato slices. Bake 10-20 minutes at 350⁰ or until crisp. Watch carefully as they burn easily.

Tortilla Chips

6   **CORN TORTILLAS**
           Cut into eighths (pie shaped). Place on non-stick cookie sheet and crisp and brown in a 350⁰ oven for 15 to 20 minutes.

           These are nice crisp chips minus all the fat and salt found in most chips. Make them ahead and recrisp in the oven if necessary.

           Take these on a picnic and pitch horseshoes for 12 minutes to burn those 60 calories.

27

Cornbread

Makes 24 small servings

50 Calories per serving

2	C.	**CORNMEAL**
1	C.	**BUTTERMILK**
2	T.	**HONEY**
1		**EGG YOLK**

Process cornmeal in food processor until fine. Then sift before measuring. Combine with next three ingredients and mix well. Set aside.

4	**EGG WHITES**

Whip until stiff but not dry. Fold egg whites into cornmeal mixture. Pour into an 8'' x 8'' baking pan. Bake 20 minutes or until brown on top.

This is wonderful with the chile recipe in this book. Spread a little low calorie butter on it for a special treat. Freeze the leftovers.

Play a little friendly volleyball for 10 minutes and you won't wind up wearing this cornbread on your hips.

Creative Crepes

Makes 6 crepes   **45 Calories per serving**

1/4	C.	**WATER**
1/3	C.	**NON-FAT POWDERED MILK**
2		**EGGS**

Blend until well mixed. Heat small crepe pan and pre-heat broiler. Add enough batter to cover the bttom of the pan. Cook over medium heat until set.

Brown top under broiler. Turn out of pan by inverting pan. HANDLE THESE CREPES GENTLY AS THEY ARE DELICATE.

Even though this recipe was included in my other publications, I felt that it belonged in this book, too. It is one of my basic recipes. The crepes freeze well and, as I'm sure you know, any leftover looks and tastes better in a crepe.

Serve them as an elegant fruit filled dessert.

Play table tennis after dinner for 10 minutes and you'll burn the calories in one crepe.

Date Nut Bread

Makes 2 small loaves   100 Calories per slice

3/4	C.	**DRY SHERRY**
1	tsp.	**BAKING SODA**
1	C.	**CHOPPED PITTED DATES**

Heat sherry. Sprinkle baking soda over dates and pour hot sherry over mixture. Cool.

2		**BEATEN EGGS**
1	tsp.	**VANILLA**
1/2	C.	**MASHED BANANA**

Combine, add to date mixture and mix well.

1 3/4	C.	**WHOLE WHEAT FLOUR**
1	tsp.	**LOW SODIUM BAKING POWDER**
1/2	C.	**CHOPPED WALNUTS**

Combine & stir into date mixture. Pour into two small loaf pans, lined with foil. Bake at 350º 50-60 minutes. Cool and cut 24 slices per loaf.

This is the best date nut bread I've ever eaten. I make large batches of it at Christmas time and give it as gifts. Notice that it has no sugar! The dates, mashed banana & vanilla make it sweet enough for almost anyone.

Enjoy 20 minutes of tennis doubles and you've burned the calories in a piece of this bread.

Eleanor's Easiest Bread

Maks 1 loaf (32 slices)   35 Calories per slice

1	T.	**YEAST**
1/3	C.	**WATER** (luke warm)
1	tsp.	**HONEY**

Combine in food processor and leave to activate the yeast.

3	C.	**WHOLE WHEAT FLOUR**
1	T.	**SESAME SEEDS**

Place in a quart glass measuring cup in a 425⁰ oven to heat the flour

1	C.	**WATER** (luke warm)
1 1/2	T.	**MOLASSES**

Combine in a 1 cup glass measuring cup with a pouring lip. Using the pulsing action on the food processor, add the flour mixture and the molasses mixture, alternately, until your bread dough begins to form a ball and pulls away from the sides of the processor bowl. Pull the dough (it will be sticky) from the processor with a spoon into a non-stick sprayed loaf pan. Sprinkle with sesame or poppy seeds and leave in a warm place to allow the dough to rise (1/2 hour). Bake at 425⁰ for 50 minutes or to brown. Turn out of pan and cool on a rack or bread board.

This bread is 'easiest' because it only takes 10 minutes to get it into your bread pan and it can rise while you do other food preparation. So, do treat yourself, your family and guests to homemade bread, often.

Spend a half an hour writing letters to burn the calories in a slice of bread.

Orange-Oat Muffins

Makes 24 muffins   75 Calories per muffin

3 1/2 C.   **ROLLED OATS**
1 1/2 C.   **FINELY GRATED CARROT**
            Combine in a large mixing bowl.

1/2   C.   **CHOPPED DATES**
1/4   C.   **RICE FLOUR**
1/8   tsp. **CORIANDER**
            Mix to coat dates with rice flour and blend into oat mixture.

1   C.   **ORANGE JUICE**
2   **EGGS**
1   tsp. **VANILLA**
            Add dry ingredients and mix well.

Using non-stick (sprayed) tins form 24 muffins. Bake at 375º for 45 minutes until brown.

This recipe, which I developed specifically for spa guests with wheat and/or milk allergies, turned out to be a favorite with everyone. Enjoy one of.these with some cantelope or grapefruit for a high energy breakfast.

Get out and hoe that garden for 15 minutes to burn 75 calories.

Whole Wheat Popovers

Makes 18 to 24 small popovers

18 = 35 Calories per popover
24 = 26 Calories per popover

1	C.	**WHOLE WHEAT FLOUR**

Sift before measuring. Use scant measure. Pre-heat oven to 450º. Warm flour in oven.

3   **EGGS**

Beat with electric mixer in large bowl until light yellow.

1   tsp.   **HONEY**
1 1/2   C.   **SKIM MILK**
1   tsp.   **SAFFLOWER OIL**

Put honey, milk and oil in blender and mix. Add flour and blend. Pour blender contents into eggs with electric mixer running.

Using non-stick (sprayed) muffin tins, form 24 popovers. Place in pre-heated (450º) oven for 20 minutes. Shut off oven and let stand for another 20-30 minutes until crisp. Do not open door during baking.

Remove and cut a slash in each popover to allow steam to escape.

These can make a simple soup and salad meal seem special. Freeze or refrigerate the leftovers and reheat them in the oven to recrisp.

You can burn off one popover by biking at a rate of 10 miles per hour for just 5 minutes.

EXERCISING IS MORE FUN THAN DIETING.

Albondegas Soup

Makes 6 Cups   100 Calories per cup

1/2	lb.	**GROUND VEAL**
3/4	C.	**COOKED BROWN RICE**
1 1/2	T.	**CHOPPED PARSLEY**
1		**GARLIC CLOVE** (minced)
1	T.	**FRESH MINT** (chopped)
1		**EGG**

Combine and mix well. Form into 1/2" balls. Place on a cookie sheet and brown in 400° oven for 15 minutes.

1	Qt.	**TOMATO JUICE**
3/4	C.	**RED WINE**
3/4	T.	**JENSEN'S BROTH POWDER**

In a soup kettle, Combine and bring to a boil.

1/2	C.	**BELL PEPPER** (chopped)
1		**MEDIUM ONION** (chopped)
1		**GARLIC CLOVE** (minced)
3/4	tsp.	**OREGANO**
1 1/2	C.	**TOMATOES** (chopped)

Add to boiling stock. Reduce to simmer and cook for 1/2 hour. Add meatballs and cook for 15 minutes.

Serve topped with fresh snipped parsley or chives.

This is a Mexican meatball soup that we serve as a first course at the Spas. It usually preceeds our very popular tostada. Make some extra meatballs for your freezer and serve them with Italian sauce for a quick and easy dinner.

If you get out on the golf course and carry your own clubs, you'll burn the calories in a cup of this soup in 20 minutes.

Cream of Carrot Soup

Makes 6 servings   **70 Calories per cup**

2	C.	**JENSEN'S BROTH POWDER STOCK**

Bring to a simmer.

3	C.	**CUT CARROTS**
1	C.	**CHOPPED ONION**
1/4	C.	**CHOPPED CELERY**
1/2		**SMALL LEAF**

Add to stock and cook until carrots are tender. Remove from heat, cool and remove bay leaf. Puree soup in blender.

For cold soup

1	C.	**BUTTERMILK**
		PINCH OF DILL WEED
2	T.	**LOW-FAT COTTAGE CHEESE**
1	tsp.	**LEMON JUICE**

Add to blender and puree until smooth. Serve in chilled cups with a dollop of yogurt or low calorie sour cream.

For hot soup

1	C.	**WATER**
1/2	tsp.	**CURRY POWDER**
3/4	C.	**BUTTERMILK**

Add to blender contents and return to the soup kettle. Heat through.

You might serve this hot the first night and serve the cold version the next night.

Paddle your canoe for just 10 minutes to burn the calories in a cup of this soup.

Lentil-Barley Meal in a Bowl

6 Main dish servings (2 C.)   200 Calories per serving

1	C.	BARLEY
1	C.	LENTILS
1	C.	CHOPPED ONION
1/4	C.	JENSEN'S BROTH POWDER*
3	Qts.	WATER*
		DASH PARMESAN CHEESE

Combine all ingredients in a large kettle. Bring to a boil. Reduce to simmer and cook one hour or until lentils and barley are tender.

Serve with a sprinkle of parmesan cheese in heated bowls.

*Recipe items with an asterick can be substituted with 3 quarts of a good stock. As this sits the liquid will be absorbed. It will then make a good stew. Simply add mushrooms and any vegetables that you desire.

As a soup add broth powder and water to suit you personally for taste and consistency.

This great tasting combination of lentils and barley is a complete protein. With a Pita Bread salad you have a great but simple meal. Keep some in your freezer for those "no cook" nights.

Take an after dinner walk for 35 minutes at a brisk clip (15 minute miles) and you'll walk off the whole bowl of soup.

Mushroom-Tofu Soup

Makes 6 Cups   70 Calories per serving

1	Qt.	**WATER**
		Add **CHICKEN BONES**
1		**BAY LEAF**
1 1/2	tsp.	**DR. JENSEN'S BROTH POWDER**
1	tsp.	**MARJORAM**
1	tsp.	**THYME**
1	tsp.	**BASIL**

Make stock by simmering for 3 to 4 hours in a large soup pot. Remove the bones and bay leaf.

1 1/2	C.	**CELERY** (chopped)
2	T.	**ARROWROOT**
2	T.	**WATER**

Add to pot and simmer for 1/2 hour. Dissolve the arrowroot in the water and add slowly while stirring. This will thicken the soup.
Add and Heat.

1/2	C.	**WHITE WINE**
3	C.	**MUSHROOMS** (sliced)
1 1/2	C.	**SLICED TOFU** (drain well before slicing)

Serve in heated bowls with parsley freshly cut from your garden . . .or the market variety.

Just 10 minutes of singles tennis will burn the 70 Calories.

37

Quickest Minestrone

Makes 6 Cups   **100 Calories per cup**

3	C.	**SOUP STOCK**
3	C.	**TOMATO JUICE**
1	C.	**CHOPPED ONION**
1		**GARLIC CLOVE** (pressed)
1/4	tsp.	**MARJORAM**
1/2	tsp.	**BASIL**
1/2	tsp.	**OREGANO**

Combine in soup kettle and bring to a boil.

2	oz.	**PASTA** (noodles, fettuccini, spaghetti or what you have on hand)
1	Qt.	**CUT VEGETABLES, INCLUDING ZUCCHINI, POTATO, CARROT, EGGPLANT, & BELL PEPPER** (or what you have)

(Fresh is best, but use frozen when time is short.)

Add vegetables and potato to soup and simmer until tender.

1/2	C.	**COOKED KIDNEY BEANS**

Add and mix well. Taste and add Jensen's broth powder as needed.

Serve in heated bowls topped with a sprinkle of Parmesan cheese. What could be better after the last ski run of the day.

And 16 minutes of downhill cruising will burn up a bowl of this soup.

Sherried Green Pea Soup

Makes 6 Cups

100 Calories per cup

6	C.	**WATER**
4	C.	**FRESH OR FROZEN GREEN PEAS**
3	T.	**JENSEN'S BROTH POWDER**
1	tsp.	**HONEY**
1/4	C.	**SHERRY**
1/4	C.	**NON-FAT POWDERED MILK**

Combine and heat but do not let boil. Set aside to cool. Then puree the mix in a blender and reheat without boiling.

Serve immediately in heated bowls with a bit of low-cal sour cream on top. Add a sprinkle of dill weed.

A cup of this would taste awfully good after cross country skiing and each 15 minutes of skiing burned the calories in a cup of this soup.

Vichysoisse

Makes 6 Cups   80 Calories per cup

4	C.	**LEEKS** (trimmed)
1	T.	**WHITE VERMOUTH**

Cut leaks into 1/2'' sections. Bring vermouth to a boil and saute leeks until limp (approx. 10 minutes).

1	C.	**POTATO** (peeled and sliced)
2	C.	**CAULIFLOWER** (sliced)
4	C.	**CHICKEN STOCK**

Combine in a pot and bring to a boil. Then lower the heat and simmer until the cauliflower and potato are tender (about 20 minutes).

1 1/2	tsp.	**JENSEN'S BROTH POWDER**
1/4	C.	**BUTTERMILK**
1	tsp.	**DRIED DILL WEED** (ground in mortar & pestle)

Combine and slowly stir into soup. Remove from heat and cool.

Serve in chilled cups and garnish with 1 tsp. FRESH CHOPPED CHIVES. If the soup seems too thick, add more buttermilk.

A ten minute session of square dancing will burn a cup of this soup and that's a lot more fun than dieting.

40

Broccoli Salad

Makes 6 servings   **40 Calories per serving**

3   C.   **FRESH CUT BROCCOLI**
            Steam broccoli until barely tender, then chill.

1/2   C.   **TOMATO**
            Wash and dice tomato.

1   T.   **GREEN ONION** (chopped)
1   T.   **PARSLEY** (snipped)
            Toss with broccoli and tomatoes.

1/4   C.   **CREAMY MAYONNAISE**
            (see SAUCES, DRESSINGS, DIPS & SPREADS)
            Toss with broccoli mixture and chill. Serve on a bed of lettuce as a first course
            salad.

Broccoli is such a wonder food that we should serve it often. Steam twice as much
as you need for dinner and make this colorful salad the next night. Broccoli is super
low in fat and very high in fiber, vitamin C and Beta Carotene . . . to say nothing of
the fact that it tastes good.

Work on your needlepoint for about 10 minutes and you'll burn the calories in one
serving of this salad.

41

Crab Stuffed Artichoke or Tomato

Makes 8 servings   145 Calories per serving

8		**ARTICHOKES**

Cut about an inch from the tops of the artichokes to remove the thorns.

Steam or boil the artichokes until tender (45 min.-1 hr.). Cool. Remove the centers, spread the leaves and chill.

1	C.	**CRAB MEAT** (shredded)
2	C.	**LOW-FAT COTTAGE CHEESE**
1/3	C.	**CREAMY MAYONNAISE** (see SAUCES, DRESSINGS, DIPS & SPREADS)
2	T.	**GREEN ONION** (minced)
2	T.	**PARSLEY** (finely chopped)
1/3	C.	**CELERY** (chopped fine)
2	T.	**BELL PEPPER** (chopped fine)

Combine and fill artichoke with 1/2 cup of crab mixture.

Place artichoke on lettuce leaf and garnish with lemon wedges and tomato slices.

This is a sure winner with spa guests and will be equally successful with your guests. If you can't get artichokes, make the crab mixture and stuff a tomato. I, personally, find artichokes more exciting.

How about 20 minutes of water skiing for a fun way to burn your lunch calories?

42

Creamy Cucumber Mold

Makes 6 servings   50 Calories per serving

1 1/4	C.	**CUCUMBER** (peeled and coarsely chopped)
6		**THIN SLICES OF CUCUMBER**

Prepare chopped cucumbers and set aside in large bowl. Prepare sliced cucumbers and place in ice.

1/2	T.	**GELATIN**
1/4	C.	**WATER**

Sprinkle gelatin on water to soak and then stir and dissolve over low heat.

1	C.	**LOW-FAT COTTAGE CHEESE**	1/2	tsp.	**RED WINE VINEGAR**
1	oz.	**MOZZARELLA CHEESE**	1	T.	**LEMON JUICE**
2	T.	**CHOPPED GREEN ONION**	1	tsp.	**SAFFLOWER OIL**
1/4	tsp.	**ONION POWDER**	1/4	tsp.	**GARLIC POWDER**
1	T.	**PARSLEY**			

Combine in food processor and process until smooth. Add and blend in gelatin. Add this mixture to the chopped cucumbers and mix gently.

1		**EGG WHITE**

Whip the egg white until stiff and fold into the cucumber mixture. Spread into 1 qt. mold or put in individual molds. Garnish with cucumber slices and serve on a lettuce leaf. Top garnish with a sprig of parsley.

When I tasted the original cucumber mold at the home of dear friends who are true gourmet cooks, it was so delicious that I wanted to eat it all. When I asked for and received the recipe, I was glad I had stopped at seconds. The ingredients included whipped cream, mayonnaise and creamed cheese.

This is my low calorie version of that wonderful dish using ingredients from CREAMY MAYONNAISE and CREAMY CHEESE. I also substituted whipped egg white for whipped cream. The next time you think a recipe is too high in fat, try doing some substituting of your own.

Spend 5 minutes on your exercycle at a good clip and you've burned the calories in a salad serving.

Cauliflower-Beet Salad

Makes 6 servings   35 Calories per serving

2   C.   **CAULIFLOWER FLOWERETTES**
1 1/2   C.   **BEETS** (sliced)
                Steam cauliflower tender-crisp. Steam beets until tender.

1/4   C.   **SCALLIONS** (chopped)
1/4   tsp.   **OREGANO**
                Toss with vegetables in salad bowl.

1/4   C.   **CIDER VINEGAR**
2   T.   **LEMON JUICE**
1   tsp.   **HONEY**
Combine, pour over vegetables and toss. Chill and serve on a purple cabbage leaf. If not available use lettuce.

The idea for this salad comes from a Mexican cookbook. It's a pleasing combination to both the palate and the eye and a very good opportunity to utilize leftovers.

Have a good time on the dance floor doing 7 minutes of the good old foxtrot and this salad is burned up.

44

Green Bean Salad

Makes 6 servings   **35 Calories per serving**

1 1/2	C.	**FRESH GREEN BEANS** (second choice frozen)
1	C.	**HALVED CHERRY TOMATOES**
1/2	C.	**CHOPPED RED ONION**

Cut beans in 1/2'' sections and steam until tender. Refrigerate to chill. Then toss with tomato, onion and dressing.

Dressing

2	T.	**SAFFLOWER OIL**
1/4	C.	**RED WINE VINEGAR**
1		**GARLIC CLOVE**
1/2	T.	**OREGANO**
1/4	T.	**BASIL**

If you use frozen green beans don't cook them. Just thaw and mix. How easy can it be? This is also another good way to use leftovers. Every time you reheat a vegetable it looses valuable nutrients, so make it a rule to use leftover cooked vegetables in salads.

Fifteen minutes spent catching up on some desk work will burn the calories in a serving of this salad.

45

Green Pea Salad with
Curried Orange Yogurt Sauce

Makes 6 servings   50 Calories per serving

1/2	C.	**LOW-FAT YOGURT**
1/3	tsp.	**CURRY POWDER** (to taste)
1	T.	**DRIED ONION FLAKES**
1	T.	**ORANGE JUICE CONCENTRATE**

Combine and mix well.

1 12 oz. pk.**TINY FROZEN PEAS**

Toss yogurt mixture with frozen peas and thaw at room temperature or place peas in a collander and run cold water over to thaw. Drain well and toss with yogurt mixture.

Serve on a bed of greens as a first course or in a lettuce cup as an attractive addition to almost any entree.

This couldn't be easier and you can burn the whole 50 calories by raking leaves for 10 minutes. Just think! You'll have a cleaner yard and a trimmer figure.

46

Marinated Carrot Salad

Makes 6 servings   **35 Calories per serving**

3	C.	**CARROTS**

Slice into thin pennies and steam until barely tender. Place in a bowl.

1/4	C.	**TOMATO SAUCE**
2	T.	**MINCED ONION**
2	T.	**RED WINE VINEGAR**
1	tsp.	**HONEY**

Combine in saucepan. Bring to a boil, then lower heat and simmer for 5 minutes. Pour sauce over carrots and toss. Cover and chill.

Serve on a lettuce leaf and garnish with a sprinkle of chopped parsley or chives.

This is my decalorized version of a good but high calorie, high sodium carrot salad. Try it . . . You'll like it.

If you play a game of billiards after dinner, you burn the calories in a serving of this very good salad.

47

Marinated Tofu Salad

1		**CAKE TOFU** (1 lb.)

Cut in 1'' cubes and spread in a single layer in a shallow pan.

1/4	C.	**DRY SHERRY**	1/4	C.	**CIDER VINEGAR**
1/4	C.	**WATER**	1/2	tsp.	**GARLIC** (crushed)
1/8	tsp.	**BLACK PEPPER**	2	tsp.	**SAFFLOWER OIL**
2	tsp.	**HONEY**	Pinch of		**ANISE** (ground)
1/4	C.	**TAMARI SOY SAUCE**			

Combine for marinade and pour over tofu. Cover and refrigerate for several hours or overnight. Turn tofu gently 2 or 3 times.

1	**CARROT**
2	**CELERY STICKS**
1	**BELL PEPPER**

Clean and cut into matchstick pieces.

1		**SCALLION** (chopped)
1/2	C.	**CABBAGE** (chopped fine)

Toss gently with vegetables, cover and refrigerate for one hour.

Combine tofu and marinate with the vegetables and serve on a purple cabbage leaf . . . or lettuce.

If you've been wanting to try cooking with tofu, this is a good recipe to start with. It's easy as well as being nutritious and delicious. Combine this salad with soup or a sandwich and you've got a great meal!

15 minutes of calisthenics will be good for your muscle tone as well as burning the 80 calories in a serving of this salad.

Pasta Salad

Prepare early in the day

Makes 8 servings 150 Calories per cup

| 8 | oz. | **SALAD MACCARONI** |
| 1 | T. | **JENSEN'S BROTH POWDER** |

Add to boiling water and cook until done (8-10 minutes). Drain and rinse with cold water. Drain again and place in a bowl.

1/4	C.	**CHOPPED OLIVES**	1	tsp.	**GARLIC POWDER**
1/2	C.	**WINE VINEGAR**	1	tsp.	**BASIL**
1/2	C.	**TOMATO JUICE**	1/2	T.	**GRATED ONION**
1	tsp.	**OREGANO**	1/2	T.	**PARSLEY** (snipped)

Grind oregano, garlic powder and basil in mortar and pestle and add to other ingredients.

1		**BELL PEPPER** (in 1/4'' cubes)
2	C.	**CARROTS** (sliced)
2	C.	**CAULIFLOWER** (cut in small flowerettes)

Put peppers, carrots and cauliflower in steamer and steam until tender and crisp.

| 1/2 | C. | **MUSHROOMS** (sliced) |
| 4 | | **ARTICHOKE HEARTS** (cut in 1/4s) |

Add to steamed vegetables.

Toss all vegetables with pasta and dress. Chill and serve. These amounts are for a main dish serving. Smaller amounts make a fine first course.

Have a Pasta Salad for lunch and burn it up on a late afternoon jog (15 minutes at 5+ miles per hour). You'll burn calories faster for several hours afterward and feel wonderful all evening.

49

Salad Nicoise

Makes 6 servings   215 Calories per serving

6	C.	**MIXED GREENS**
2 CANS		**TUNA** (water pack — small)
3	C.	**GREEN BEANS** (cooked)
2		**POTATOES** (steamed in skins)
3		**ARTICHOKE HEARTS** (cut in quarters)
2		**MEDIUM TOMATOES** (cut in wedges)
2		**HARD BOILED EGGS** (sliced)
6		**ONION RINGS** (thin sliced, chilled in cold water)
6		**MUSHROOMS** (thinly sliced)
6		**PARSLEY SPRIGS**
1	C.	**PASTA SALAD DRESSING**

Arrange all ingredients in an attractive display on a bed of greens with the tuna in the center. You can make one large platter and let your guests serve themselves or prepare individual salads.

You'll find the Pasta Salad dressing in this section.

This is The Oaks' and The Palms' version of this classic salad. Our guests enjoy it and so will yours.

Take them all out for a walk after lunch and you'll have some great conversation as well as making sure those luncheon calories are burned rather than stored as fat. Walk at a rate of 3 miles per hour for 45 minutes.

50

Shrimp Slaw Supreme

Makes 8 servings   **210 Calories per serving**

6	C.	**GREEN CABBAGE** (shredded)
8		**EGGS** (hard boiled)
1	lb.	**SALAD SHRIMP** (cooked & chopped fine)
1	C.	**CREAMY MAYONNAISE**

Combine dressing, egg and shrimp. Toss with cabbage and chill.

This is an unusual salad which I first tasted at a potluck. It travels very well so keep it in mind to take to your next potluck.

Ride your bike to the potluck (20 minutes at 13 miles per hour) and you'll burn 210 calories before you even eat the salad.

Shrimp Stuffed Papaya

Makes 6 servings   180 Calories per serving

3   **PAPAYAS**
           JUICE OF 1 LEMON
           Halve, seed and peel the papaya. Sprinkle the papaya with lemon juice and chill.

1   lb. **BAY SHRIMP**
           Thaw shrimp and keep cold.

1   tsp. **SAFFLOWER OIL**
1   T.   **SCALLION** (minced)
1   T.   **CURRY POWDER**
1/2   C.   **LOW-FAT YOGURT**
1/2   **RIPE BANANA** (mashed)
           To make the dressing simply heat the oil and scallions. Stir in curry to make a paste, then stir the paste into the yogurt and mashed bananas. Mix well.

Pile shrimp into papaya halves and top with an ounce of dressing. Garnish with cucumber and lemon.

This is an elegant luncheon dish. The hardest part is finding ripe papayas. If yours are not quite ripe, rub the cut and seeded fruit with a little honey and steam or microwave to just heat it through. This will give it that good ripe taste and texture.

Enjoy an afternoon swim for 20 minutes without stopping and you'll feel fresh and alive. You will also have burned the calories in this exceptional luncheon dish.

52

Tabouli

Makes 6 servings

1/2	C.	**BULGUR WHEAT**
1	tsp.	**JENSEN'S BROTH POWDER**
1	C.	**WATER**

Bring water and bulgur to boil in a large pot. Remove from the heat and let it sit for at least an hour. Drain off any remaining liquid and chill the bulgur.

1	C.	**FRESH CHOPPED TOMATO**
1/4	C.	**CHIVES** (chopped)
1/4	C.	**PARSLEY** (minced)
1/2	T.	**FRESH MINT LEAVES** (minced)
1/2	C.	**RAW CAULIFLOWER** (grated)

Toss in a large bowl with the bulgur.

1/2	C.	**LEMON JUICE**
1	T.	**SAFFLOWER OIL**
1	T.	**GARLIC** (fresh pressed)

Combine, mix well and toss with the salad. Serve on a fresh leaf of lettuce.

Bulgur wheat is a fine complex carbohydrate and this Tabouli is wonderful. You'll never miss the extra fat calories found in most Tabouli recipes.

If you enjoy handball, you can burn the calories in a serving of this salad in just 10 minutes.

Baked Yam Puff

Makes 6 servings   **50 Calories per serving**

1 1/2 C.   **YAM** (large)
             Bake or microwave yam. Then remove, measure and puree the insides of the yam.

1   T.   **LEMON JUICE**
1   tsp.   **JENSEN'S BROTH POWDER**
1/4   tsp.   **CINNAMON**
Pinch   **DRIED DILL WEED**
             Add to yam puree and mix well.

2   **EGG WHITES**
1   tsp.   **VINEGAR**
             Whip until stiff and fold into yam puree. Spoon into individual custard cups and bake
             at 375° for 15 minutes or until brown on top.

             Yams are a wonderful source of Beta Carotene, that super booster of the immune
             system. Have them often and when you have them baked, which is easiest, prepare a
             double amount and save the puree for this dish.

             Just 10 minutes at the typewriter will puff away the calories in this.

Broiled Tomato Parmesan

Makes 6 servings   25 Calories per serving

3   **TOMATOES** (medium sized)
          Cut tomatoes in half and place on cookie sheet.

2   T.   **BREAD CRUMBS**
2   T.   **PARMESAN CHEESE** (grated)
          Combine and sprinkle 2 teaspoons of cheese mixture on each tomato half and place
          under broiler until brown.

1   T.   **PARSLEY** (chopped)
          Serve with a sprinkle of chopped parsley.

          This is fast and good. The bread crumbs are optional but they give it more
          substance. If you're in a hurry leave them out.

          Spend 6 minutes cleaning your bathroom and you've eliminated the calories ingested
          in half a broiled tomato.

Elly's Quick Vegetarian Chili

Makes 6 servings

200 Calories per serving

1	C.	**ONION** (chopped)
1		**CLOVE GARLIC** (crushed)
1	C.	**BELL PEPPER** (chopped)
1/4	C.	**CANNED GREEN CHILIES** (chopped)
2	C.	**TOMATO SAUCE**
2	C.	**CANNED KIDNEY BEANS** (drained & rinsed)
1	tsp.	**CUMIN** (ground)
1/4	tsp.	**OREGANO**

Combine in a kettle and simmer one hour or microwave in a casserole dish for 15 minutes (stir every 5 minutes).

1	tsp.	**CHILI POWDER**
1/4	C.	**DRY RED WINE**

Combine, add to chili and simmer 10 minutes or microwave for 3 minutes.

8	oz.	**TOFU** (drained well and chopped or, if frozen, thaw & crumble)

Add tofu, heat and serve.

3	oz.	**LOW-FAT CHEDDAR CHEESE** (grated)

Top each serving with cheese.

Some other toppings might include shredded lettuce, chopped fresh tomato and low-cal sour cream. Have a Chili Party and let everyone help themselves.

Rake your lawn for 45 minutes and you'll have a clean yard and a minus calorie balance after a bowl of good chili.

Fast Fettucini Primavera

Makes 6 servings   225 Calories per serving

| 4 | oz. | **SPINACH FETTUCINI NOODLES** |
| 2 | qts. | **WATER** (boiling) |

Cook fettucini in boiling water to desired degree of softness. Rinse in cold water. If you want to prepare your noodles ahead, toss them with a little Safflower Oil and refrigerate in a plastic bag. To reheat, put them in a collander and immerse in boiling water, drain and use.

1	tsp.	**BUTTER**
1/2	tsp.	**BASIL**
1		**CLOVE GARLIC** (crushed)

Stir over low heat to blend flavors.

| 1 | C. | **LOW-FAT COTTAGE CHEESE** |
| 1/4 | C. | **SKIM MILK** |

Combine in blender and process smooth. Add to the butter-garlic mixture. Cook this sauce, stirring over low heat until cheese melts.

| 2 | C. | **MIXED COOKED VEGETABLES** (leftovers or frozen) |

Add to sauce to heat through and toss with the Fettucini.

| 1 | C. | **CHERRY TOMATOES** (halved) |

Add and toss with the Fettucini and serve sprinkled with Parmesan cheese.

Catch up on your ironing and in 45 minutes you can eliminate the calories in a whole serving of pasta.

Frosted Cauliflower

Makes 6 servings   20 Calories per serving

3	C.	**CAULIFLOWER**

Break into flowerettes. Steam until just tender and keep warm.

1/2	C.	**LOW-FAT COTTAGE CHEESE**
1	tsp.	**RED WINE VINEGAR**
1	tsp.	**LEMON JUICE**
1	tsp.	**GREEN ONION** (chopped)
1	tsp.	**PARSLEY** (snipped)
1	tsp.	**PARMESAN CHEESE**
Pinch		**DRY MUSTARD**
Pinch		**DILL WEED**

Make "Frosting" by combining ingredients in blender or food processor until smooth.

1	tsp.	**PAPRIKA**

To serve, dip flowerette end of cauliflower in sauce and serve frosted side up with a sprinkle of paprika.

If you have some Creamy Mayonnaise or Low-Cal Sour Cream on hand, you won't have to make the "frosting." Just season and use.

This can be a very dramatic looking vegetable dish for your next buffet. You can also leave the steamed cauliflower whole (cut part way through stems for easy serving) and present the entire cauliflower, frosted.

Park your car and walk to the store and you'll burn 20 calories every 4 minutes.

Magic Macaroni and Cheese

Makes 6 servings   225 Calories per serving

6	oz.	**TWISTED PASTA**
2	qts.	**WATER**
2	T.	**JENSEN'S BROTH POWDER**

Bring water to a rolling boil, add macaroni and cook al dente (8-10 minutes). Drain. Place in a casserole dish.

Microwave Method: Place pasta in casserole, cover with hottest tap water, cover with vented lid. Microwave 10 minutes on high and drain.

3	C.	**LOW-FAT COTTAGE CHEESE**
1	T.	**JENSEN'S BROTH POWDER**

Combine and mix with the maccaroni.

3   oz.   **LOW-FAT CHEDDAR OR MOZZARELLA** (grated)

Sprinkle cheese over maccaroni and bake, uncovered, at 350º for 45 minutes. This works well in individual ramekins and they'll be ready in half an hour (faster in your microwave).

Ride your bike for half an hour (12 miles per hour) and you won't wind up wearing this dish on your thighs.

59

Oven-Fried Onion Rings

Makes 6 servings   **30 Calories per serving**

1	lg.	**ONION**

Peel onion and discard thin outer layers. Slice 1/4'' rounds and separate into rings.

1/3	C.	**WHOLE WHEAT FLOUR**
3	T.	**NON-FAT POWDERED MILK**
2	tsp.	**JENSEN'S BROTH POWDER**
1/4	C.	**WATER**
1		**EGG YOLK**

Combine in a large bowl and mix well.

1		**EGG WHITE**

Whip egg white until stiff and fold into batter. Fold in onion rings gently. Separate onion rings and bake on non-stick sprayed cookie sheet for 15 minutes at 400⁰ or until brown and crisp.

These may be baked a little ahead and recrisped in a hot oven before serving.

This recipe was inspired by Sheila Cluff, who is fond of Onion Rings but wanted to be able to enjoy them without the fat used in French frying. She asked me to come up with something and this is what developed. Our guests at The Oaks and The Palms really enjoy them.

You can erase those 30 calories during the 10 minutes it takes to clean your bedroom.

Pita Pizza

Makes 6 servings   200 Calories per serving

1	C.	**TOMATO SAUCE**	1/2	tsp.	**OREGANO**
1/4	C.	**BURGUNDY WINE**	1/2	tsp.	**BASIL**
1	T.	**OLIVES** (mInced)	1/2	tsp.	**THYME**
1		**GARLIC CLOVE** (pressed)	1/2	tsp.	**MARJORAM**

Combine and simmer for 1/2 hour . . . or buy a sauce without added salt or sugar.

1	C.	**ONION** (chopped)
1	C.	**BELL PEPPER** (chopped)
1	C.	**ZUCCHINI** (sliced thin)

Add to tomato sauce mixture and simmer 1/2 hour or until vegetables are just tender.

3   **WHOLE WHEAT PITAS** (small)

Split pitas in half and place on a cookie sheet. Heat under broiler to brown. Spoon half cup of vegies and sauce over each pita.

1   C.   **FRESH MUSHROOMS** (thin sliced)

Spread over vegies and sauce.

6	oz.	**MOZZARELLA** (grated)
2	T.	**PARMESAN CHEESE** (grated)

Combine and sprinkle over each pizza. Place cookie sheet with pizzas under the broiler until the cheese melts.

If you keep some sauce and vegetable mixture on hand, this is an extremely good and easy meal.

Water skiing is fun and burns 200 calories in 25 minutes.

Simple Stuffed Acorn Squash

Makes 2 servings   90 Calories per serving

1	sm.	**ACORN SQUASH**

Halve and remove seeds. Sprinkle with Jensen's Broth Powder.

1/4	C.	**ONION** (chopped)
1/4	C.	**ORANGE SEGMENTS** (chopped)

Combine and fill squash cavity with mixture. Place in a casserole, cover, and bake at 350⁰ for 45 minutes (or microwave for 15 minutes).

2	T.	**NON-FAT YOGURT** (or low-fat sour cream)

Top each serving with a tablespoon of the above.
Serve squash as an accompaniment to any chicken or fish dish.

10 minutes of doubles racquetball should more than handle the calories in half a squash.

Spinach with Onion

Makes 6 servings   **25 Calories per serving**

| 6 | C. | **FRESH SPINACH** |
| 1/4 | C. | **ONION** (minced) |

Wash and trim spinach. Combine with onion and toss together. Steam until limp.

| 1 | C. | **HARD BOILED EGG** (grated) |

Serve garnished with grated egg.

or make

Speedy Spinach with Onion

| 1 | pk. | **FROZEN SPINACH** (chopped) |
| 2 | T. | **DRIED ONION FLAKES** |

Thaw spinach and mix with onion. Heat through and garnish as above.

If you spend 3 minutes climbing stairs, instead of riding the elevator, you'll burn 25 calories.

Wild Rice Pilaf

Makes 6 servings   **60 Calories per serving**

1	T.	**TAMARI SOY SAUCE**

Put in pan and heat.

1/4	C.	**BROWN RICE**
2	T.	**WILD RICE**
1	C.	**ONION** (chopped fine)
1	C.	**BELL PEPPER** (chopped fine)

Combine in pan and "stir fry."

1	C.	**SOUP STOCK OR WATER**
1	tsp.	**JENSEN'S BROTH POWDER**

Add stock (or water) to stir fry. Bring to a simmer, cover and simmer 1 hour.

1	tsp.	**SAFFLOWER OIL**
1	C.	**CELERY** (coarsely chopped)
1	C.	**MUSHROOMS** (sliced thin)

Stir fry until just cooked tender crisp. Fold into cooked rice mixture and serve.

You might want to double or triple this recipe. It freezes well and is nice to have on hand. If you remember to soak the rice overnight, it will cook faster and your wild rice will swell and puff up more for better volume.

You can burn this dish off in 6 minutes of running at 5 miles per hour.

Zucchini Saute
and/or
Zucchini Frittata

Makes 6 servings

30 Calories per serving for Saute
165 Calories per frittata

6   C.   **ZUCCHINI**
1   tsp.   **DRIED DILL WEED**
Shred zucchini and sprinkle with dill. Using stir fry method, saute in a non-stick sprayed pan until just done. Do not overcook and, also, cook the zucchini at the last possible moment. The color should remain bright green.

2   T.   **PARMESAN CHEESE**
Serve with a sprinkle of Parmesan cheese.

This is simple and one of the most attractive and delicious ways to serve zucchini that I know.

Frittata

If you want to make a main dish out of it simply mix 4 eggs with a cup of cottage cheese. Add a pinch of oregano and basil, pour the mix over your lightly sauteed zucchini and you'll have a ZUCCHINI FRITTATA. Sprinkle some grated Mozzarella over the top place under the broiler and when your frittata is set and your cheese is melted, cut into wedges and serve with sliced tomato for a fine lunch or supper.

A half an hour of digging in your vegetable garden cancels out your lunch.

Cashew Chicken with Tofu

Makes 8 servings

235 Calories per serving

1	lb.	**TOFU**

Drain well and cut in 1'' cubes.

3	T.	**TAMARI SOY SAUCE**	1	tsp.	**FRESH GINGER** (minced)
1 1/2	T.	**SHERRY**	1	tsp.	**FRESH GARLIC** (minced)

Combine for marinade and put tofu in sauce for several hours. Turn and baste frequently.

1/2	C.	**RAW CASHEWS** (chopped)

Toast cashews and set aside.

2		**CHICKEN BREASTS** (cooked, skinned & cubed)

Add chicken to tofu in marinade.

1	T.	**SAFFLOWER OIL**	2	C.	**ONIONS** (halved and sliced)
4	C.	**CELERY** (sliced diagonally)	3	C.	**BROCCOLI** (sliced diagonally)

Stir-fry vegetables in oil until onion is transparent. Use wok or large pan.

2	C.	**MUSHROOMS** (whole or halved)
2	C.	**SPINACH** (shredded)

Add mushrooms, spinach, tofu and chicken and cover the pan.

1/4	C.	**MARINADE**
1	tsp.	**ARROWROOT**

Mix marinade and arrowroot. Stir into vegetables to thicken the sauce. Coat vegetables, chicken and tofu.

Serve topped with toasted cashews.

This is easy to do if you prepared your vegetables and chicken while you put away your food. If you like Chinese food, you'll love this.

How about some volleyball? A half an hour could just about obliterate the calories in a serving.

Chicken Fricasse

Makes 6 servings

200 Calories per serving

3		**CHICKEN BREASTS** (skinned)
1/2	C.	**WHITE WINE**
1	T.	**GARLIC POWDER**
1	T.	**JENSEN'S BROTH POWDER**
1	tsp.	**PAPRIKA**
3	C.	**CARROTS**
2	C.	**POTATO** (unpeeled)
2	C.	**CELERY** (cut)

Place all ingredients in covered roasting pan. Cook for 2 hours at 350º or combine in a crockpot and simmer all day.

1	T.	**ARROWROOT**
1/2	C.	**ORANGE JUICE**

Combine and stir into Fricasse to thicken gravy.

I like the crockpot method for this good dish because it's so pleasant to come home on a chilly evening and smell dinner cooking.

If you biked home from work, at 10 miles per hour for half an hour, you dropped the calories in your dinner entre.

Chicken Relleno

Makes 6 servings   210 Calories per serving

1/2	C.	**ONIONS** (chopped)
1		**GARLIC CLOVE** (pressed)
1	C.	**TOMATO SAUCE**
1	tsp.	**BASIL** (heaping)
1	tsp.	**OREGANO** (heaping)
1	tsp.	**CHILI POWDER**

Combine in pot and simmer for 1 hour.

3		**WHOLE CHICKEN BREASTS** (cooked, skinned and sliced)
1 small can		**WHOLE GREEN CHILIS** (seeded)
1	C.	**MOZZARELLA CHEESE** (grated)

Layer chicken, green chilis and cheese in a baking dish or into individual ramekins.
Top with sauce and bake at 350º for 1/2 hour to heat through, or heat in microwave.

A half an hour in most aerobic dance classes will more than burn the calories in this
flavorful chicken dish.

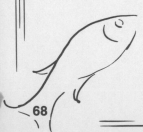

68

Crab Quiche

Makes 6 servings   **180 Calories per serving**

3   C.   **LOW-FAT COTTAGE CHEESE**
1/2   C.   **MOZZARELLA** (grated)
1/4   C.   **GREEN ONION** (chopped)
1/2   C.   **FRESH PARSLEY** (snipped)
             Pre-heat oven to 350°. Combine ingredients in a bowl and mix.

3   **EGGS**
             Beat eggs until light and fold into crab mixture.

1   C.   **CRAB MEAT** (shredded)
             Fold crab into cheese mixture and spread the whole thing in your quiche dish which
             has been sprayed with non-stick spray.

1/3   C.   **PARMESAN CHEESE** (grated)
             Top with Parmesan Cheese. Bake for 45 minutes or until brown on top.

             Sliced tomato tastes like it was made for this wonderful quiche!

             Eating raises your metabolism and if you'll take an easy 45 minute walk a half hour
             after your meal, you'll burn the calories in this quiche and then some.

Fish Fillets Baked In Yogurt Sauce

Makes 6 servings   **115 Calories per serving**

1 1/2 lb.   ORANGE ROUGHY (SOLE, FLOUNDER OR COD), CUT IN 6 PIECES
Arrange on a broiler pan.

1/4   C.   NON-FAT YOGURT
1   T.   HORSERADISH
1   T.   LEMON JUICE
2   tsp.   DRY MUSTARD
2   T.   PARMESAN CHEESE (grated)
Combine in a small bowl and stir with a spoon. Spread yogurt mixture over fish fillets
in a thin, even layer. Bake covered in a 350⁰ oven for 12 minutes or until fish just
flakes.

If you take care not to overcook this, you'll have moist, tender and flavorful fish. So
easy and so good!

I think running in place is boring but it will burn the calories in a serving of this fish
in 15 minutes. (Run in front of your TV set.)

Oven "Fried" Chicken Breasts

Makes 6 servings   **190 Calories per serving**

1/2	C.	**ORANGE JUICE**
1/4	C.	**LEMON JUICE**
1	tsp.	**TAMARI SOY SAUCE**

Combine in baking dish.

3   **CHICKEN BREASTS** (halved and skinned)

Place in juice, bone side up. Cover and bake at 350⁰ for 1 hour or microwave 1/2 hour at medium. Remove chicken and boil or microwave pan juice to reduce to 1/4 the volume. Glaze each chicken piece with reduced pan juice.

2	T.	**PARMESAN CHEESE** (grated)
1	tsp.	**PAPRIKA**

Combine and sprinkle over each chicken breast. Brown in a hot oven at 450⁰ or under the broiler.

This is just as good cold as it is hot. Take some on your next fishing trip. You'll burn a piece of chicken in just a little over half an hour of fly fishing.

71

Polla Picata

Makes 4 servings   210 Calories per serving

1	lb.	**TURKEY BREAST** (sliced thin)
1	tsp.	**OLIVE OIL** & 2 tsp. **SAFFLOWER OIL** (mixed)

Heat oil and quickly saute turkey on each side until white. Remove and place on cookie sheet in serving portions or place each serving in a ramekin.

1/4	C.	**LEMON JUICE** (fresh)
1/4	C.	**DRY VERMOUTH**
1/2	T.	**ARROWROOT**
4		**LEMON SLICES** (very thin)

Combine, put in pan turkey was cooked in and cook and stir until thickened.

1 1/2	C.	**MUSHROOMS** (sliced)
2	T.	**FRESH PARSLEY** (snipped)

Add and cook mushrooms until just tender. Do not cook them until they shrink. Spoon mushrooms and gravy over each serving of turkey and serve sprinkled with 1 tsp. of fresh snipped parsley. Each serving should have a lemon slice. This may be assembled ahead and quickly reheated.

Many markets now sell sliced raw turkey breast. It looks and tastes a lot like very expensive veal. I served this dish as veal to my husband and he loved it! (He thinks he doesn't like turkey.)

Invest 45 minutes in wall papering your hall and be relieved of about 210 calories.

Quick Turkey Parmesan

Makes 6 servings   **175 Calories per serving**

1	lb.	**RAW TURKEY BREASTS** (sliced thin)
1/3	C.	**PARMESAN CHEESE** (grated)
1	tsp.	**GARLIC POWDER**

Combine garlic powder and grated cheese. Lay the turkey pieces flat on a bread board. Sprinkle with the cheese mixture and pound with a mallet until cheese is absorbed. Turn meat and repeat.

2	T.	**OLIVE OIL**

Heat oil in skillet and saute the turkey until just done (the meat will turn white).

Combine this with a baked potato and large green salad for a satisfying, quick and easy meal.

Does your lawn need mowing? Pushing a light power mower for 35 minutes will erase all that turkey, so you won't wind up wearing it around your middle.

Turkey Divan

Makes 6 servings   **200 Calories per serving**

3	C.	**BROCCOLI** (cut & lightly steamed)

Place in a baking dish.

12	oz.	**COOKED TURKEY BREAST**

Cut in 1/2'' cubes.

2	C.	**CELERY** (sliced)
1/4	C.	**ONION** (chopped)

Mix with turkey.

1/4	C.	**CREAMY MAYONNAISE** (see Dressings, Sauces, etc.)
1	tsp.	**SOY SAUCE**

Combine, toss with turkey mixture and pile lightly on top of broccoli.

1/2	C.	**LOW-FAT MOZZARELLA** (grated)
2	T.	**PARMESAN** (grated)

Combine and sprinkle over turkey mixture. Bake at 350º for 10 to 15 minutes to just heat through or microwave for 5 minutes.

A good use of leftovers. If you leave out the broccoli, you'll have a HOT TURKEY SALAD.

Rope jumping is a fine aerobic exercise. Twenty minutes of it will eliminate 200 calories.

Turkey Kabob

Makes 6 servings

Makes 6 servings   200 Calories per serving

1 1/4 lbs. **RAW TURKEY** (cut in 1 oz. chunks)
            Place in a shallow baking dish.

1   C.   **PINEAPPLE JUICE**
1/3   C.   **TAMARI SOY SAUCE**
1/3   tsp. **FRESH GINGER ROOT** (grated)
            Combine and pour over turkey chunks to marinate for 1 hour or longer.

12 1'' pieces of **ZUCCHINI**
12 chunks of   **PINEAPPLE**
12 1'' pieces of **ONION**
            Arrange turkey, zucchini, pineapple and onion on skewers and bake at 375º for 30
            minutes.

            For your next barbecue, let your guests skewer and cook their own kabobs. It's easy
            for you and fun for them.

            And then get up a game of touch football and in 20 minutes those 200 calories per
            serving will be unloaded.

Turkey Tofu Stroganoff

Makes 8 servings   325 Calories per serving

1	T.	**ONIONS** (minced)	1/2	T.	**HONEY**
1/2	tsp.	**GARLIC** (crushed)	1/4	C.	**TAMARI SOY SAUCE**
1	T.	**DRY SHERRY**			

Saute onion and garlic in half the sherry. Add the rest of the wine, honey and tamari. Bring to a simmer and set aside.

1   lb.   **TOFU** (well drained and cut in cubes)
Place in shallow 8" baking pan and pour marinade over. Turn Tofu, brown under the broiler and set aside.

1   lb.   **TURKEY BREAST** (cooked & shredded)
Set aside.

water + rice Flour

| 2 | C. | **LOW-FAT COTTAGE CHEESE** | 1 | T. | **LEMON JUICE** |
| 1/2 | C. | **BUTTERMILK** | 1 | T. | **JENSEN'S BROTH POWDER** |

Blend smooth and stir. Heat in double boiler.

veg

6   C.   **RAW MUSHROOMS** (sliced)
2   T.   **SHERRY**
Stir-fry mushrooms in sherry to just heat through and set aside.

Rice & Noodles

3/4   lb.   **SPINACH NOODLES**
1/4 gallon   **WATER** (boiling)
Cook noodles tender, drain and rinse.

Layer noodles, turkey, tofu, mushrooms & sauce. Garnish with fresh parsley. This can also be served as an excellent vegetarian dish by simply doubling the tofu and omitting the turkey. This saves about 25 calories per ounce.

Play some fast racquet ball for half an hour to liquidate the calories in a serving of this dish.

Ambrosia

Makes 6 servings   **50 Calories per serving**

1 1/2	C.	**FRESH PINEAPPLE** (crushed)
3/4	C.	**BANANA** (sliced)
3/4	C.	**ORANGE SLICES** (broken)

Combine in a large bowl. Put 1/2 cup servings in sherbet glasses.

| 2 | T. | **COCONUT** (grated) |

Toast coconut and sprinkle 1/2 tsp. on each serving.

This simple combination of fresh fruit tastes special and it's got lots of fiber, vitamin C and Beta carotene. So enjoy it often!

15 minutes of golf, even if you use a power cart, will burn the 50 calories in a serving of this dessert. Have seconds and play for a half an hour!

Apple Brown Betty

Makes 6 servings   70 Calories per serving

1	C.	**BRAN**
2	T.	**WHEAT GERM**
1 1/2	T.	**CINNAMON**
1/2	T.	**SESAME SEEDS**

Crush sesame seeds in mortar and pestle. Combine ingredients and mix well in bowl.

| 1 | | **LEMON** (juice) |
| 5 | | **APPLES** (cored and sliced thin) |

Spray 8'' baking dish with non-stick spray. Sprinkle a layer of bran mixture on the bottom of the dish. Layer thinly sliced apple and sprinkle with lemon juice. Layer more bran mixture. Top with thinly sliced apple and sprinkle with lemon juice. Cover tightly with foil. Bake at 350⁰ for 1 1/2 hours. Chill, cut into squares and serve.

This is very good with a little yogurt or low calorie sour cream. You'll be amazed at how sweet this tastes even with no sugar.

Take some along on your sailboat and you'll burn 70 calories in 15 minutes (handling a small boat).

78

Carob-Peanut Butter Syrup (and Mousse)

Makes 1 cup   16 Calories per tablespoon

2	T.	**HONEY**
2	T.	**CAROB POWDER**
1	tsp.	**ARROWROOT**

Combine in a saucepan and stir over low heat.

3/4   C.   **HOT WATER**
Add to pan and stir mixture for 3 minutes or until thickened.

1   T.   **PEANUT BUTTER**
Stir into syrup and remove from the heat.

1/2   tsp.   **VANILLA**
Stir into syrup and chill.

Microwave Method: Combine all ingredients and microwave 2 minutes on high.
Remove and stir.

This is a delicious topping for ice cream. However, we usually use it in a mousse at
The Oaks and The Palms.

To make the Mousse, fold 1/4 C. syrup into 1 C. of the NON-FAT WHIPPED CREAM*
and serve in sherbet glasses. Top with a little syrup.

This will cost 100 calories for a half cup portion and it's worth every calorie.

*SAUCES, DRESSINGS, DIPS & SPREADS

Chiffon "Pumpkin" Pie

Makes 8 servings   55 Calories per serving

| 1 | C. | **BUTTERNUT SQUASH OR PUMPKIN** |

Steam until very soft, then puree in blender.

2	T.	**HONEY**
2	tsp.	**MOLASSES**
1	tsp.	**CINNAMON**
1		**EGG YOLK**
Pinch		**GINGER**
Pinch		**ALLSPICE**

Add to squash mixture in blender and mix well.

| 2 | | **EGG WHITES** |

Whip until it forms peaks. Fold squash mixture into whipped egg whites. Pour into pie pan. Bake at 350° for 1 hour and cool.

Wonderful for a Holiday or any day. Top with non-fat yogurt or NON-FAT WHIPPED CREAM (see SAUCES, DRESSINGS, DIPS AND SPREADS).

Play your guitar or violin for 10 minutes after dinner and you'll cancel the calories in your dessert. (Unburned calories are apt to be stored as fat.)

Eight Precious Pudding

Makes 6 servings   90 Calories per serving

1/4	C.	**BROWN RICE**
1/2	C.	**WATER**

Cook until tender.

1	C.	**APPLE** and/or **PEAR** (chopped)

Add apple for last 15 minutes, if boiling rice for 1 hour. If you are microwaving add for last 5 minutes. Remove from heat.

1/2	C.	**BANANA** (chopped)
1/2	C.	**PINEAPPLE** (crushed)
1/2	tsp.	**CINNAMON**
1 pinch of		**GINGER**

Add to rice and mix well. Refrigerate to chill. Gently fold rice into WHIPPED CREAM (see SAUCES, DRESSINGS, DIPS AND SPREADS).

Serve in sherbets garnished with date sugar or sliced strawberry with mint.

Play croquet for a half hour after dinner and you'll burn up a whole serving of this delicious pudding. Try serving it for breakfast for a nice change of pace.

Fruit Whip

Makes 6 servings
2 1/2 Cups

50 Calories per serving

1/2	C.	**NON-FAT DRY MILK**
1/2	C.	**ICE COLD FRUIT JUICE** (orange, prune, pineapple, berry)

Combine in a deep bowl and whip to hold soft peaks.

2	tsp.	**LEMON JUICE**

Add and whip until mixture holds stiff peaks.

1 to 2 T.	**FROZEN ORANGE OR APPLE CONCENTRATE**

Taste, whip and add concentrate to taste.

Heap in sherbet glasses and serve as a Bavarian Cream. This whip can also be used as a topping. Use this within 2 hours after preparation. What a great way to save the fat and sugar calories in whipped cream!

Need some painting done? Every 10 minutes that you paint will burn the calories in one of these desserts.

Orange Oat Cookies

Makes 2 dozen   45 Calories per cookie

2   C.   **ROLLED OATS** Rice Flour
1   C.   **CARROT** (grated fine)
             Combine in a large mixing bowl.

1/4   C.   **DATES** (chopped) Prunes, Raisins
2   T.   **RICE FLOUR**
Pinch   **CORIANDER** OK
             Combine to coat dates with flour and mix into oat mixture.

1   C.   **ORANGE JUICE** pineapple juice
1   **EGG**
1/2   tsp.   **VANILLA** Almond
             Combine, add to dry ingredients and mix well. Drop by tablespoons on non-stick
             sprayed cookie sheet and flatten with a fork. Make the cookies as large and thin as
             possible. Bake at 350º for 35 minutes or until brown.

             This will produce a soft chewy cookie. If you want a crisp cookie, turn off the oven
             and leave the cookies in the oven until they cool.

             Carry a couple of these high energy goodies in your pocket the next time you plan to
             really attack the slopes with some aggressive downhill skiing. You'll burn a cookie in
             about 5 minutes.

Persimmon Fruit Cake

Makes 4 large loaves or 8 small loaves   75 Calories per small slice

3	C.	**PERSIMMON PULP**
1/4	C.	**SWEET WINE**
2	C.	**WALNUTS**
5	C.	**DRIED FRUIT** (raisins, dates, figs, pineapple, banana and/or apple)
1/2	C.	**NON-FAT POWDERED MILK**
2	T.	**BAKING SODA**

Combine in a large bowl.

3	C.	**WHOLE WHEAT PASTRY FLOUR**
1	tsp.	**CINNAMON**
1	tsp.	**ALLSPICE**

Combine, stir into persimmon mixture and mix these ingredients well.

Line loaf pans with foil. Fill 3/4 full of batter. Place these pans in a larger pan with a little water in the bottom. Cover with a large sheet of foil. Bake 1 1/2 hours. Remove cover and check the water. Bake another 1/2 hour. Remove the cakes, in their foil liners, from their pans and cool on a rack. These can, later, be wrapped in Sherry soaked cheese cloth or just foil.

These cakes keep for a long time in the refrigerator or forever in the freezer.

You can save some calories if you substitute fresh chopped apple for some of your dried fruit.

Spend 15 minutes sweeping your porch and walks and you'll use all the calories in a piece of cake.

84

Popcorn

HONEY CORN (heaping 1/2 C.)   20 Calories per serving
CARMEL CORN (heaping 1/2 C.)   20 Calories per serving
HONEY JACK (heaping 1/2 C.)   30 Calories per serving
SEASONED CORN (heaping Cup)   25 Calories per serving

Honey Corn

4	C.	**POPCORN** (air popped)
2	T.	**HONEY**
1	tsp.	**VANILLA**

Place honey and vanilla in a container over low heat or microwave to liquify. Pour mixture over popcorn and toss with two large spoons to coat.

Carmel Corn (my favorite)

1	T.	**PEANUT BUTTER**

Add to Honey Corn mixture and liquify.

Optional additions to Carmel Corn or Honey Corn are:

Toasted Sunflower Seeds
Coconut
Sesame Seeds

Seasoned Corn

1	C.	**POPCORN** (air popped)
2	T.	**JENSEN'S BROTH POWDER** and/or **CURRY POWDER, CHILI POWDER, GARLIC POWDER OR ONION POWDER.**

Combine in a large sack and shake vigorously.

Popcorn, popped without fat is a super snack for anyone interested in being fit. Popcorn has lots of fiber and it's very filling.

You can burn the 20-30 calories in a small serving of this by cleaning up the kitchen after preparing the popcorn.

Sherried Pear

Makes 6 servings   **50 Calories per serving**

3   **PEARS** (medium size — ripe)
          Cut pears in half and remove seeds and stems. Place cut side up on cookie sheet
          (close together).

2   T.   **SHERRY WINE**
1   tsp. **VANILLA**
          Combine wine and vanilla. Pour teaspoon of wine mixture over each pear and let sit
          for an hour. Turn pears cut side down and bake at 350º for 45 minutes. Place pears
          cut side up on dessert plate and serve. These can be served chilled, room
          temperature or warm.

2   T.   **NON-FAT YOGURT**
          Mix yogurt with pan juice and serve the pears topped with the mixture.

          This is very simple and exceptionally good. Peeled pears look pretty, but as a busy
          person, you don't have time to peel pears and why waste the fiber in the peels?

          Mountain climbing can be exciting fun and burns 50 calories in 5 minutes.

86

Winter Fruit Compote

6		**PRUNES**
1 1/2	C.	**APPLE CHUNKS** (with peel)
1	C.	**PEAR CHUNKS** (with peel)
1/4	C.	**RED GRAPES** (halved & seeded)
1 small		**BANANA** (sliced)
2	T.	**LEMON JUICE**
1	tsp.	**NUTMEG**

Toss fruit in a baking dish with lemon juice and nutmeg. Bake at 350° 20 minutes or microwave on high for 5 minutes.

1/2	C.	**NON-FAT YOGURT**

Serve warm topped with dash of yogurt and a sprinkle of nutmeg.

Easy — quick — good — and good for you. What more could you ask for?

Shovel a little snow for 8 minutes and along with your clean walk you have worked off your dessert.

Notes

Notes